Mother's LOVE IS...

Mina Parker

Conari Press

First published in 2008 by Conari Press,
an imprint of Red Wheel/Weiser, LLC
With offices at:
500 Third Street, Suite 230
San Francisco, CA 94107
www.redwheelweiser.com

ISBN: 978-1-57324-406-0
Library of Congress Cataloging-in-Publication Data available upon request.

Cover and text design by Kristine Brogno.
Typeset in Liorah and Gotham.
Cover and text illustrations © iStockphoto.

Printed in Hong Kong
SS
10 9 8 7 6 5 4 3 2 1

A mother's love is big as a house, deep as an ocean, constant as the stars. A mother's love is all encompassing, all knowing, and all forgiving. It is home. And yet, as big as it is, a mother's love remembers all the details and knows the littlest things can be the most important—like how much chocolate in the milk, when to offer advice and when to be still, and just the right squeezing that makes the perfect hug. From the biggest moments down to the sweetest nothings, a mother's heart stands at the ready to comfort, encourage, inspire, protect, and, most of all, love.

Seeing is different than being told.

AFRICAN PROVERB

Mother's LOVE *shows us the way.*

The strength of motherhood
is greater than natural laws.

BARBARA KINGSOLVER

Mother's COURAGE *can move mountains.*

When you are a mother,
you are never really alone in your thoughts.
A mother always has to think twice,
once for herself and once for her child.

SOPHIA LOREN

Mother's
WISDOM
holds
you close.

A mother understands
what a child does not say.

JEWISH PROVERB

Mother's
INTUITION
knows your heart.

It is not until you become a mother
that your judgment slowly turns
to compassion and understanding.

ERMA BOMBECK

Mother's LOVE *forgives most anything.*

Sweater, n.: garment worn by child
when its mother is feeling chilly.

AMBROSE BIERCE

Mother's
LOVE
keeps you warm.

Mother's love is peace.

It need not be acquired, it need not be deserved.

ERICH FROMM

Mother's
PATIENCE
never fails.

A mother is the truest friend we have when trials heavy and sudden fall upon us.

WASHINGTON IRVING

Mother's
LOVE
shelters and
protects.

The mother's heart is the child's schoolroom.

HENRY WARD BEECHER

Mother's
LESSONS
build our
foundations.

Cleaning the house while your kids
are still growing is like shoveling
the walk before it stops snowing.

PHYLLIS DILLER

Mother's
WORK
is never done.

My mother had a slender, small body,
but a large heart—a heart so large
that everybody's joys found welcome
in it, and hospitable accommodation.

MARK TWAIN

Mother's HEART *is home.*

No one in the world can take the place
of your mother. Right or wrong, from her
viewpoint you are always right. She may
scold you for little things, but never
for the big ones.

HARRY TRUMAN

Mother's
LOVE
sees us at our best.

A little girl, asked where her home was,
replied, "where mother is."

KEITH L. BROOKS

Mother's LOVE *is big as a house.*

Motherhood has a very humanizing
effect. Everything gets reduced
to essentials.

MERYL STREEP

Mother's
HEART
knows what
matters.

A mother's arms are made of tenderness
and children sleep soundly in them.

VICTOR HUGO

Mother's WARMTH *is better than a blanket.*

All that I am, or hope to be, I owe to my angel mother.

ABRAHAM LINCOLN

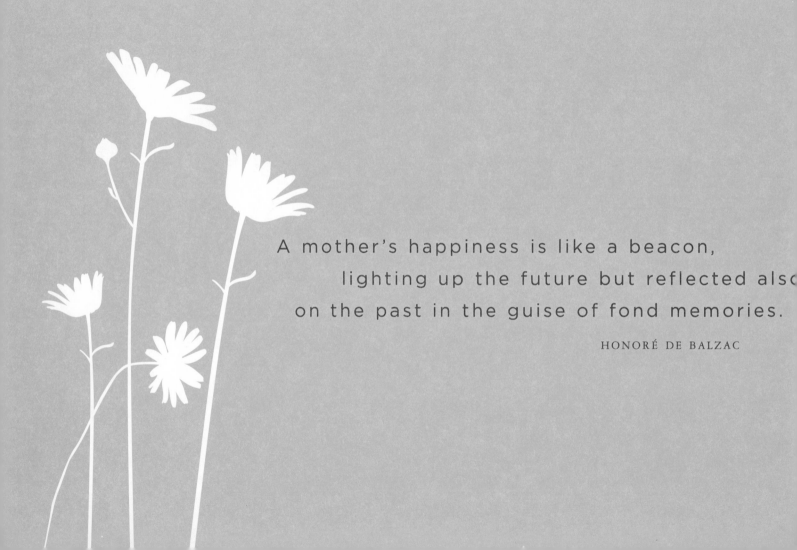

A mother's happiness is like a beacon,
lighting up the future but reflected also
on the past in the guise of fond memories.

HONORÉ DE BALZAC

Mother's
JOY
spans lifetimes.

Mother—that was the bank where
we deposited all our hurts and worries.

T. DEWITT TALMAGE

Mother's
COMFORT
makes us rich.

Mother's love grows by giving.

CHARLES LAMB

Mother's
GIFTS
grow and
multiply.

My mother wanted me to be her wings,
to fly as she never quite had the courage
to do. I love her for that.

ERICA JONG

Mother's LOVE *watches us soar.*

My mom is a never-ending song in my heart of comfort, happiness, and being. I may sometimes forget the words but I always remember the tune.

GRAYCIE HARMON

Mother's
LOVE
sings in

harmony.

She never quite leaves her children at home,
even when she doesn't take them along.

MARGARET CULKIN BANNING

Mother's LOVE *is always there.*

The best academy, a mother's knee.

JAMES RUSSELL LOWELL

Mother's WIT *keeps us on our toes.*

The heart of a mother is a deep abyss
at the bottom of which you will always find forgiveness.

HONORÉ DE BALZAC

Mother's
COMPASSION
knows
no bounds.

A mother is a mother still,
The holiest thing alive.

SAMUEL TAYLOR COLERIDGE

Mother's
LOVE
feeds the soul.

One of the oldest human needs is having
someone to wonder where you are when
you don't come home at night.

MARGARET MEAD

Mother's LOVE *never sleeps—* especially with babies and teenagers.

It kills you to see them grow up.

    But I guess it would kill you quicker if they didn't.

BARBARA KINGSOLVER

Mother's
REST
is fleeting.

The moment a child is born, the mother
is also born. The woman existed, but
the mother, never. A mother is something
absolutely new.

RAJNEESH

Mother's DREAMS *grow and thrive.*

A mother is not a person to lean on but
a person to make leaning unnecessary.

DOROTHY C. FISHER

Mother's WISDOM *makes us strong.*

There was never a great man who had not a great mother—
it is hardly an exaggeration.

OLIVE SCHREINER

Mother's
LOVE
demands our best.

Biology is the least of what
makes someone a mother.

OPRAH WINFREY

Mother's LOVE *is broad and deep.*

The best conversations with mothers
always take place in silence, when
only the heart speaks.

CARRIE LATET

Mother's
WISDOM
whispers
the truth.

Some mothers are kissing mothers
and some are scolding mothers,
but it is love just the same, and
most mothers kiss and scold together.

PEARL S. BUCK

Mother's LOVE *is gentle and firm.*

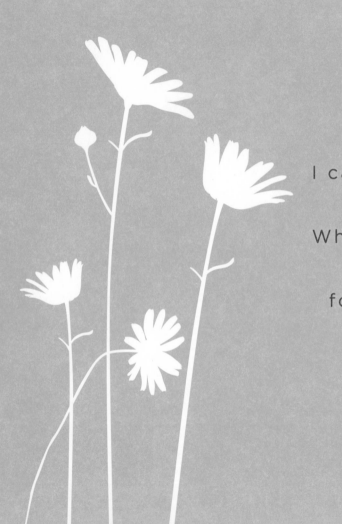

I cannot forget my mother.
She is my bridge.
When I needed to get across,
she steadied herself long enough
for me to run across safely.

RENITA WEEMS

Mother's
COURAGE
sustains us.

My mother bore me glad and
sound and sweet, I kiss her feet!

MARGUERITE WILKINSON

Mother's GIFTS *are for life.*

A mother's arms are more comforting than anyone else's.

DIANA, PRINCESS OF WALES

Mother's
HUG
feels like home.

The hand that rocks the cradle
is the hand that rules the world.

W.R. WALLACE

Mother's
LOVE
*is in a class
by itself.*

Any mother could perform the jobs of several air traffic controllers with ease.

LISA ALTHER

Mother's LOVE *is never too busy for hugs and kisses.*

To Our Readers

Conari Press, an imprint of Red Wheel/Weiser, publishes books on topics ranging from spirituality, personal growth, and relationships to women's issues, parenting, and social issues. Our mission is to publish quality books that will make a difference in people's lives—how we feel about ourselves and how we relate to one another. We value integrity, compassion, and receptivity, both in the books we publish and in the way we do business.

Our readers are our most important resource, and we value your input, suggestions, and ideas about what you would like to see published. Please feel free to contact us, to request our latest book catalog, or to be added to our mailing list.

Conari Press
An imprint of Red Wheel/Weiser, LLC
500 Third Street, Suite 230
San Francisco, CA 94107
www.redwheelweiser.com

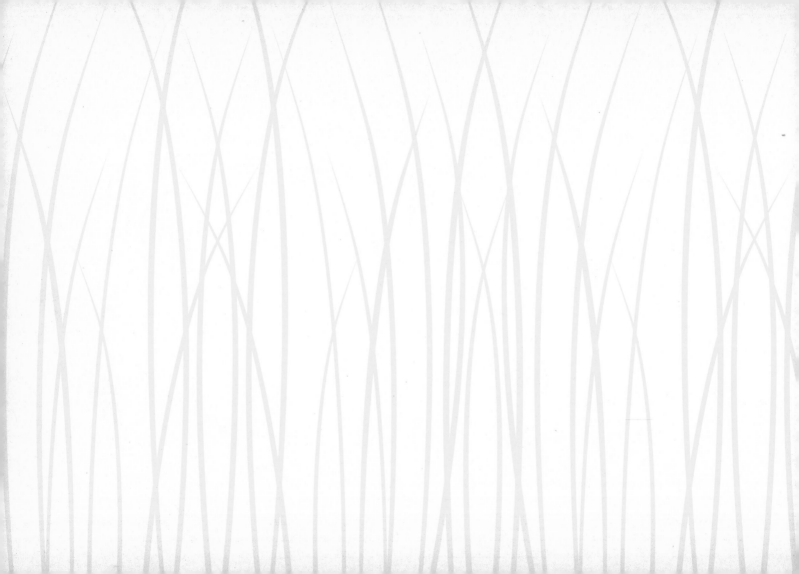